VOL. 6

HAL•LEONARD®

VIOLIN

PLAY-ALONG

AUDIO
ACCESS
INCLUDED

Classic
CHRISTMAS SONGS

T0087039

PLAYBACK+
Speed • Pitch • Balance • Loop

To access audio visit:
www.halleonard.com/mylibrary

Enter Code
5589-6903-3893-5360

Tracking, mixing, and mastering by Jake Johnson
Violin by Jerry Loughney
Additional violin ("Merry Christmas, Darling") by Chris Wagoner
Guitars by Doug Boduch
Bass by Tom McGirr
Keyboards by Warren Wiegratz
Drums by Scott Schroedl

ISBN 978-1-5400-9732-3

HAL•LEONARD®

Visit Hal Leonard Online at
www.halleonard.com

Contact us:
Hal Leonard
7777 West Bluemound Road
Milwaukee, WI 53213
Email: info@halleonard.com

In Europe, contact:
Hal Leonard Europe Limited
42 Wigmore Street
Marylebone, London, W1U 2RN
Email: info@halleonardeurope.com

In Australia, contact:
Hal Leonard Australia Pty. Ltd.
4 Lentara Court
Cheltenham, Victoria, 3192 Australia
Email: info@halleonard.com.au

HAL•LEONARD®

VIOLIN
PLAY-ALONG

AUDIO
ACCESS
INCLUDED

Frosty the Snow Man

Words and Music by Steve Nelson and Jack Rollins

1. Frost - y the snow man was a jol - ly hap - py soul, with a
3. *See additional lyrics*

corn - cob pipe and a but - ton nose and two eyes made out of coal.

Frost - y the snow man is a fair - y tale they say. He was

made of snow but the chil - dren know how he came to life one day. There

must have been some mag - ic in that old silk hat they found, for when they placed it
See additional lyrics

4. *See additional lyrics*

Additional Lyrics

3. Frosty the snow man
   Knew the sun was hot that day,
   So he said, "Let's run and we'll have some fun
   Now before I melt away."
   Down to the village
   With a broomstick in his hand,
   Running here and there all around the square,
   Sayin', "Catch me if you can."

Bridge He led them down the streets of town
   Right to the traffic cop,
   And he only paused a moment
   When he heard him holler, "Stop!"

4. For Frosty the snow man
   Had to hurry on his way,
   But he waved goodbye sayin', "Don't you cry,
   I'll be back again some day."

Here Comes Santa Claus
(Right Down Santa Claus Lane)

Words and Music by Gene Autry and Oakley Haldeman

1. Here comes San - ta Claus! Here comes San - ta Claus! Right down San - ta Claus
2., 3., 4. *See additional lyrics*

Lane! Vix - en and Blitz - en and all his rein - deer are

pull - ing on the rein. Bells are ring - ing, chil - dren sing - ing,

all is mer - ry and bright. Hang your stock - ings and say your pray'rs, 'cause

San - ta Claus comes to - night. San - ta Claus comes to - night.

Additional Lyrics

2. Here comes Santa Claus! Here comes Santa Claus!
Right down Santa Claus Lane!
He's got a bag that is filled with toys
For the boys and girls again.
Hear those sleigh bells jingle, jangle,
What a beautiful sight.
Jump in bed, cover up your head,
Santa Claus comes tonight.

3. Here comes Santa Claus! Here comes Santa Claus!
Right down Santa Claus Lane!
He doesn't care if you're rich or poor,
For he loves you just the same.
Santa knows that we're God's children;
That makes ev'rything right.
Fill your hearts with a Christmas cheer,
'Cause Santa Claus comes tonight.

4. Here comes Santa Claus! Here comes Santa Claus!
Right down Santa Claus Lane!
He'll come around when the chimes ring out;
Then it's Christmas morn again.
Peace on earth will come to all
If we just follow the light.
Let's give thanks to the Lord above,
Santa Claus comes tonight.

Jingle Bell Rock

Words and Music by Joe Beal and Jim Boothe

(There's No Place Like)
Home for the Holidays

Words and Music by Al Stillman and Robert Allen

Let It Snow! Let It Snow! Let It Snow!

Words by Sammy Cahn
Music by Jule Styne

Merry Christmas, Darling

Words and Music by Richard Carpenter and Frank Pooler

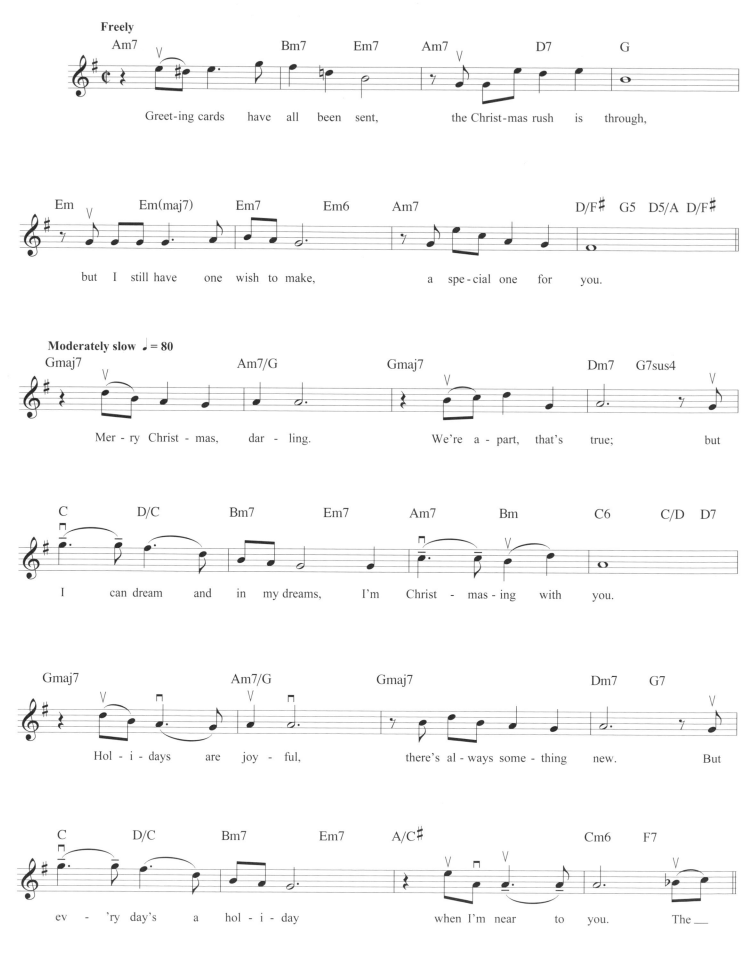

Rudolph the Red-Nosed Reindeer

Music and Lyrics by Johnny Marks

they nev - er let poor Ru - dolph join in an - y rein - deer games.

Then one fog - gy Christ - mas Eve, San - ta came to say,

"Ru - dolph, with your nose so bright, won't you guide my sleigh to - night?"

Then how the rein - deer loved him as they shout - ed out with glee;

"Ru - dolph, the red - nosed rein - deer, you'll go down in his - to -

ry!" you'll go down in his - to -

ry!"

Silver Bells

from the Paramount Picture THE LEMON DROP KID
Words and Music by Jay Livingston and Ray Evans

Additional Lyrics

2. Strings of street lights, even stop lights
   Blink a bright red and green,
   As the shoppers rush home with their treasures.
   Hear the snow crunch, see the kids bunch,
   This is Santa's big scene,
   And above all the bustle you hear: